100 Ways to to Make Money in Pri$on

Baby Auk

Cadmus Publishing
www.cadmuspublishing.com

Published by Cadmus Publishing LLC
www.cadmuspublishing.com
Haledon, NJ

ISBN: 978-1-63751-360-6

Note: None of these ideas pertain to gambling, intoxication, selling/ buying illegal substances, oppressing physically or mentally to anyone. Please follow prison rules and guidelines.

Please be aware that some of these resources may have changed their address, or may not contact you A.S.A.P.

Dear Never Broke Again,

This booklet is the cure to being broke. It's a lot of people in prison who wants to see someone sink while knowing they have the power to help them. Well, guess what? Not anymore. You are now holding 100 Ways to Make Money in Prison legally all by yourself. I have personally used a lot of these ideas and actually created most of them to get me where I'm at (six figures). Yeah, you are gonna lose some friends, some even gonna laugh at you because you're not destroying yourself no more like them. I walked around prison for years following these 100 ways. Only bought what I needed, saved a lot, stayed focused, and didn't look for problems, only looked for opportunities. Your life didn't stop just because you came to prison. You just gotta stop watching TV and instead watch your account grow.

Da Prisonaire

YOU GOTTA DO WHAT'S BEST FOR YOU,
NOT THEM.

1. Rent MP3 Player/Music/Tablet

Just like Rent-A-center but a different kind of formula. Buy an MP3 player if you don't already have one. Purchase all the NEW music that comes out. Make sure you get gospel, R&B, rock-n-roll, and rap. You may spend about $90 - $150 for the player/tablet and buy music every two weeks after the renter pays you and brings it back. It's a lot of you right now you have music on your systems and just sit and listen to it all day and waste money on songs. Why not rent it out to someone who can't afford to purchase the whole setup?

2. Room Service

Each dorm, unit, or housing area has at least 50 rooms/cells in it. Whether you realize it or not, we are actually living in a prison hotel. The correctional officers serve us food. If you call them, they come. Even our cells are set up like a cheap motel. But one thing they're not going to do is clean your rooms for you. So, guess what? This is where you come in. Make you a special chemical, get shampoo, a towel and wash rag. The prison already supplies you with water, a broom, and bucket. Go walk around and spread the word. Even do monthly specials where you will clean and wash a whole room four times a month. Oh yeah, and just to spice things up, spray a lil smell-good when you finish.

3. Coffee Shots

It's not too many people that's incarcerated that doesn't drink coffee. A lot of guys can't even function without it or they will get a headache. I actually heard that coffee is good for the heart. We don't want to see anyone with a headache, right? So, go purchase a couple bags of coffee. I think Keefe is the most popular around $2.50 to $3.50 for a 3-ounce bag. You'll get about 40 to 50 shots using a white plastic spoon. Try not to run out because you'll never have too much. One stamp each.

4. Text Messages

If your facility allows you to have a text messaging service, why not think like an entrepreneur and make $$ off it? I know it be a lot of inmates bothering you asking to send a text out for them. So, turn it into a business. Charge a few stamps to send a message and the reply is free. Use your customer's money to pay for your service. Make sure you let them know no illegal transactions or assaulting texts that could lead you to a disciplinary shot.

5. RAFFLE BOARD

You can become an owner in 10 minutes. No, I'm serious. Okay, listen up. Grab an all-white piece of typing paper. Draw a board of 100 squares with numbers 1 through 100. Charge $1 a square for inmates to buy, don't matter the limit of how many squares they buy. But once it's filled up, it's over with. Make sure you put their name in each square they purchase. Okay, now look. Before you start, make sure you come up with a name for your board. And at the top put "$1 wins you $60," and actually, it does because once you fill up the whole board you should have $100 in your possession. You pay the winner $60, and you keep $40. How you declare the winner is by putting all the numbers in a hat or etc. in front of everyone, and as you grab out the numbers you cross out their box on the board and the last box standing will win. You can do this two times a week.

6. SOUR TWIZZLERS

An all-time favorite. Purchase as many packs of Twizzlers you can afford. Also purchase a couple boxes of green apple Kool-Aid. It must be green apple. Now open a pack of Twizzlers. It should be around 20 in one pack. Out of one pack you should be able to cut around 65-80 pieces. Then you sprinkled one pack of Kool-Aid all over the pieces. Next you bag up about 7 to 10 pieces in each and now you're ready to distribute. Two to three stamps.

7. BANANA PUDDING

Everyone can't make banana pudding, just like everyone can't make macaroni and cheese. You got to have that special touch. But if you are that special one, then what are you waiting for? Invest in yourself. A couple small bowls, vanilla wafers, cookies, free bananas, creamer, sugar, and your secrets you'll never tell no one. Then after you're done, let it sit on ice until ready to sell. Take the $$ you make and reinvest again. Take preorders and build a damn pudding factory.

8. INSTITUTION JOB

For some reason, nobody doesn't wanna work now days. They want everything handed to them. Life doesn't work like that. Some institution jobs may pay more than others, but you gotta start at the bottom to get where you want to be. Don't focus on the pay, focus on the position you have that could possibly benefit you. For example, a kitchen job. Now you can save your food in your locker. Recreation job. Now you can work-out and learn about equipment. Yard crew. Walk around picking up trash, you also losing weight and able to advertise things you're selling. Always look for opportunities and always remember it's not always about the pay, but about the advantage your position gives you to make more money or learn from.

9. PRISON FOOT LOCKER

Just stop for a second. Look around you. I can guarantee that there's no one around you walking bare-footed. Everybody needs shoes. So, put yourself in a position to fulfill the need. Go buy up any type of shoes as long as they're not falling apart. Get different sizes, colors, work-out shoes, fancy ones, and etc. Buy low so you can make a profit. Start spreading the word that you buy used/new shoes and watch, you'll create a shoe outlet.

10. CUT HAIR

A lot of you in prison have talent but are devaluing it. If you know how to cut hair, then what are you waiting for? Let me guess. You don't have clippers. So what? Use some good razors. Guys are always looking for a trim or shape up. Start today. Let everyone know you are the new barber. It's enough room for everyone to get money, so I don't wanna hear it's already someone doing it.

11. FIX ELECTRONICS

When I first seen guys do this it blew my mind. It's like having a mechanic on the outside. If your radio, headphones, watch, or etc. is broken, take it to the guy who is good. Are you the person? Open up your shade tree cell. You'll never run out of clientele.

12. COLD SODAS

It's nothing like having a cold soda to drink, especially coming in the unit from rec or a hot sunny day or just to go with your meal. Start your business today. Get a couple cases to start off with. Make sure it's different kinds. If you don't have a bucket, special cooler, or trash bag to keep the ice in to put the sodas on, just use your sink. Most cases are around $4 to $5, so just do the math. You'll make double or more even selling at $1 to $1.50 each.

13. NACHO DIPS

Game changer. Take a styrofoam tray and cut the lid off. Then you cut off the big eating part and leave only the two slots left. So, you should be left with only two sides. Put some nacho chips in both sides and some squeeze cheese on top of the chips. Quick and easy. Ready to go. Start with two cheese bottles $6 and three bags of nacho chips $6, $12 total investment.

14. DISHWASHER

Laugh if you want to, but they're laughing broke. Just think about how many people eat meals a day. A lot of people are lazy or don't have time to wash their dishes. Make it your job. Break your ego.

15. INVESTMENTS

Now, if you have a lil money saved on your prison account and feel the need to just sit around and do nothing, I got something for you. Wanna earn interest on it? Grab a 50-cent stamp and envelope. Write this company and say, "I want to learn more about your service." Pilgrim

Cross Group B, Port Orchard, WA 98366.

16. STAMPS FOR CASH

You have a lot of services that are starting to let you send in brand new stamps and they will put the money on your account at their value. Here are a couple resources: 1) Great Goods, PO Box 888, Lakeworth, FL 33460; 2) P.S.E. 1077 N. Willow Ave. #107-405, Clovis, CA 93611.

17. STOCKS

If you are into stocks and stopped because you're in prison or are learning about them, it's legal ways you can still buy/sell shares through mail. Here are two companies that will assist you: 1) Computer Shareholders, PO Box 505000, Louisville, KY 40233, 1-800-298-0146; 2) Bureau of the Public Debt, PO Box 7015, Parkersburg, WV 26106.

18. SELL PEN PALS

Always remember to think like an entrepreneur. I know there are a lot of great pen pals out there. People that have been in my life for years come from pen pals. Guys lose them because they try to take advantage of them or have the wrong intentions from the start. When you got a good one, hold on to him/her and help other people find one. Here is a company that sells lists of pen pals. You can order the lists and sell them individually and become known as the matchmaker. Their address is: PO Box 2515, Nyssa, OR 97913. Send $6 or one book of stamps.

19. WORKOUT MEMBERSHIPS

If you have experience and methods on how to help people lose weight, all you have to do is start your own workout class. Charge each inmate by the month around $15 to $20. You must supply healthy snacks, drinks, and prison equipment like weight bags and etc., and before you know it, you'll have a waiting list!

20. IRON CLOTHES

Prison Fly is what they call someone who is always creased up 24/7 for pics, visits, or daily. You can become the cleaners. Make a special spray for starch and schedule dates inmates have occasions. They may look good wearing it, but you is the man who made it happen.

21. PHONE MESSAGES

Do you not realize that you only get between 10 to 15 minutes on the phone? So, in order to deliver a message for someone is taking your time. So, charge them an item or couple of stamps. It's like shipping and handling. You're shipping your time and handling their business.

22. COMEDIAN

No, I am actually serious. Are you a natural-born funny person or have funny prison stories? Well, you can make $$ off it. Write to: Mr. Story, PO Box 60903, Philadelphia, PA 19133, and if he uses or likes your funny stories, they will pay you for it.

23. ENTERTAINER

If you're a movie writer or want to get your voice heard and have no $$ to start with, don't worry. Contact UBF Scholarship Foundation, PO Box 862, Bristow, OK 74010-1010. They're a nonprofit looking to put the funds up for inmates. The founder is a prisoner himself.

24. SELLING/LICENSING IDEAS

Do you have an idea or product you want to sell or license, but because you're in prison you can't effectively market it? Write to: American Intellectual Property Law Association, 2001 Jefferson Davis Highway Suite 203, Arlington, VA 22202.

25. Building Growth

I love this service. They help you with inmate banking, building credit, cash app, and re-entry. So, if you're on your way home soon and need resources, this is who you need to contact. And yes, they do all this and more while you're incarcerated. Write to: J.K.C. 1140 Cornell Street, Scranton, PA 18504.

26. Law Work

You know it's more than 2.3 million people locked up in the U.S., more than any other country. Also, more than half the cases have errors in them, and 15 percent have been getting out wrongly convicted after doing 15 or more years. If you have experience with codes and rights, what are you waiting for? People need your help and are wiling to pay for their freedom and justice. Become the prison lawyer and before you know it, you'll have a law firm inside the walls.

BAD COMPANY WILL CORRUPT GOOD CHARACTER.

27. TAFFY CANDY

The hottest commodity in prison. A quick rundown—one bag of nondairy creamer and around 8 to 10 packs of Kool-Aid. Poor the three-ounce creamer into a bag with the Kool-Aid and mix it around. Keep adding half a teaspoon of water into the mix until it's a nice kinda hard texture. Spread it out flat and cut around 100 pieces. One stamp apiece gets you about $30 off a $5 investment.

28. SUCKERS (BLOW POPS)

A great demand. You gonna need about 10 empty pill bottles, a bag of Jolly Ranchers or hard fruit candies, and some Q-Tips. Put three pieces of candy in each pill bottle, then you put the bottles in the microwave with the lids off, five at a time. Keep stopping the timer and look every 10 seconds until the candy melts. Next, take them out and stick the Q-Tips in while it's soft, then hold the sticks until the candy hardens. Lastly, pop the sucker out. $1 to $2 each.

29. THE BREAKDOWN (CHIPS)

I actually believe I was the first inmate to actually breakdown chips. Some people can't afford to buy a whole bag, so I made it to where they could be satisfied also. Just get different kinds and put a handful in little sandwich baggies. You should get about 6 to 8 small baggies out a big bag. At 2-3 stamps each you'll become big. Trust me.

30. RESELL BOOKS

Why would you buy information and then give it away? No, you sell the information as well once you get everything out of it you wanted. People misuse books all the time, so let them do it with their time, not yours. If you keep buying them and then give them away, you just became a dependent.

31. SELL COLD MILKS

Milks are free, issued out every morning at breakfast, so get up early and collect them. Bring them back to the unit and put on ice. A lot of guys don't get up so early, so make sure you have the milk for their cereal when they get up or for the ones who don't like to walk up to the hall.

32. BREAKFAST (IHOP)

The early bird gets the worm. Set it up so you can have eggs, bacon, grits, bread, and etc. Make breakfast sandwiches and give your customers an orange Hi-C drink on the side.

33. FRIED WRAPS

Quick and easy to serve. Rice, meat, cheese, vegetables, sauces, and etc. Always keep them hot and tasty. A $15 investment makes you $45. Twenty tortillas. You must stay consistent.

34. PRISON CHEF

You could either cook food and sell it or cook for other people and charge them, but they must bring all the items to make it. Start you a restaurant and take orders three times a week. Hire you some help and get to work. Why waste your talent when you can get paid off something you love to do anyways?

35. PRISON HUT (PIZZA)

It is nothing like a loaded pizza with all type of toppings. I have literally tasted a pizza that would put Papa John's out of business. See, you have individuals that only know how to make certain food. Make you a dough, some use bread, crackers, or etc. Get seasonings, sauce, cheeses, meats, vegetables, and a formula you keep a secret. Take orders and also do free delivery.

36. HAND CRAFT

If you make picture frames, cars, boats, animals, or etc. I have the right service for you. They will purchase your items and put the funds on your account. A contract also has to be signed. Write to: Sticks From the Yard, 2283 Sunset Drive, Wickliffe, OH 44092.

37. SEW CLOTHES

Do you know how to sew? If so, go buy a needle and thread from commissary. It should run you no more than $5. Make you a little written flyer and let people know your prices and etc. The inmates need you. Quit thinking you don't have a way to benefit yourself and others.

38. LAUNDROMAT

I know every facility will wash your laundry for free, but just look how they come back. Wrinkled, shrunken, and no smell good. It's nothing wrong with washing clothes. A lil secret—the washing machine is actually washing it, all you're doing is watching it, making sure it gets dried and folded. Use some good washing powder and charge by the week. (WOW)

39. WASH SHOES

Good soap, shampoo, new toothbrush to scrub, and towel. Buy some shoe polish just in case they need it. Turn bad into good and you're in business.

40. PAWN SHOP

The biggest business I ever started in prison. You want to buy low items so you can also sell cheap items. Anything that I saw with value I purchased or made value out of it. If customers pawned something and didn't pay the low interest in one week, you keep it. Remember to be fair and just.

41. TYPE CONTRACTS

Dealing with a lot of businesses and agreements rather for court or power of attorneys, you'll need some kind of contracts. So, if you know how to type let your fingers make you money.

42. BRAID HAIR

Whoever said this is a female job is a lie. This is a great, great hustle and a must-need in prison. If you know how to braid or do dreads, don't hide it. Let it be known and stack your commissary and account up. Even give monthly specials.

43. BODEGA

How can we survive without a small store around? Become an owner today. Just start small and you will grow huge. A lot of people fail at it because they don't understand supply, demand, bookkeeping, pay yourself, saving, and being a people's person all played a part of their downfall. Don't let that be you. I went from $50 to starting outside businesses off a prison bodega and so can you.

44. SELL PICTURES

Who doesn't like exclusive pics of Instagram models or etc.? Here are two services that sell cheap pics in bulk and you can resell them to fit someone's desire. Write to: 1) Kill Shot King, PO Box 81074, Corpus Christi, Tx 78468; 2) Free Prints App - Get the most popular Instagram Pics and have loved ones send them to you. They sell like hotcakes.

45. LIL JUICYS

Make you a big pitcher of Kool-Aid, about 10 ounces or more. Make sure it's nice and tasty. Get you some small baggies and pour the Kool-Aid in each one. Make sure you can tie them up okay so when it's done sit them on ice and in 20 minutes you got lil juicys.

46. ALL HYGIENE

Just like a bodega, but instead just stick to all cosmetics. Less complicated and people know where to buy only hygiene.

47. The Copier

Just wait until they see this idea. Go buy a couple copy cards around $6 to $7 each. You get 50 copies on each card. Spread the word you charge two stamps a copy, includes shipping/handling. Even give specials when you copy five or more pages. You'll triple your money and become the copy man/woman.

48. Single Cookies

It's just something about breaking things down. You'll see. Go buy some packs or bag of cookies. It has to be at least 18 or more single cookies in the bag in order to break down. Put 3 or 4 in little baggies and distribute them nonstop. Two to three stamps each.

49. Popcorn

Either buy cheddar popcorn or the microwave kind. It will be great if you had both. Get lil baggies and put both kinds together in the lil baggie and get ready to advertise your butter and cheddar enterprise. At 3 stamps each you'll kill 'em.

50. Brownies

I promise you it's so, so simple. Find some hot cocoa mix off commissary. A box is around $2. Put about four packs in a big bowl. Add some milk, just enough to make it thick, but still soft. Put the bowl into the microwave and watch it rise up like a cake. Keep your eye on it. Take it out, put peanuts or etc. on it. Cut into slices and your new business just started.

WE ALL CAN HAVE THE SAME
GOAL, BUT IT'S OUR MISSION THAT
SEPARATES US.

51. WRITE POEMS

Are you a great poem writer? If so, get paid and published in articles. Here are two resources to enter into contests and more: 1) Poete Maudit, PO Box 216, Farmersville, CA 93223; 2) Pen America Writing Program, 588 Broadway Suite 303, New York, NY 10012.

52. SELL ARTWORK

Sometimes inmates in prison don't want to pay your prices. Don't devalue yourself. Deal with services on the outside who will purchase your work from prison. Write to: Creative Freedom, PO Box 119, Williamson, WV 25661.

53. GHOST WRITER

Just like the music industry but instead do it for prisoners. People need poems, letters, grievances, and more written up. So, if you're good with your words and speech, we need you. Start letting it be known ASAP.

54. CROCHET

If you don't already know how to do it, you might as well learn. Invest $7 to buy a 35-page booklet for beginners at: E.P.S., PO Box 1717, Appleton, WI 54912, and start making money.

55. DRAW PORTRAITS

It takes time but as an artist your time is valuable. Inmates love to get portraits of loved ones, kids, and etc., and if you don't know how you can always purchase books to teach you.

56. FANCY ENVELOPES

Simple hustle. Buy a box of all-white envelopes (50-count) around $2. Trace or draw some nice designs and characters on al of them. Put one stamp on them and sell the envelopes around 4 to 5 stamps pre-stamped and fancy.

57. EYE COVERS

Guess what? You can make money off people's sleep. Just start making eye covers. For some reason, just covering your eyes really relaxes you. I use mine every night.

58. SHARK TANK

Yes, you have a lot of entrepreneurs all around you. Some are even willing to invest in some of these ideas if you show them you're serious and have a nice plan to pay them back. And vice-versa with the sharks who are looking to invest in a prisoner. Don't take advantage of them, that's a sign of weakness. If you do it correctly, you'll both benefit.

59. PILLOWS

Only if your unit or etc. allows you to have one, you could be the one to provide a cotton pillow for inmates. Some COs take them, some don't, so if you're the pillow man/woman, I guess it's more money for you.

60. TOOTSIE ROLLS

Game changer. Let me show you. Buy some hot cocoa mix and one bag of nondairy creamer. Pour about four packs of cocoa mix and the bag of creamer all in one trash bag (a small bag). Mix it all up then put lil by lil teaspoons of water in it until it gets hard. Keep pressing the bag and spreading it until it's smooth. Then cut up nice pieces like Tootsie Rolls (60 to 80 pieces). One stamp each.

61. BOTTLES OF KOOL-AID

Go buy a case of water. Empty all the water into one big container. Put about one box of Kool-Aid into the container also. Basically, make you some good, sweet Kool-Aid. Now all the empty water bottles you have, fill up the bottles. Put the bottles on ice and do your thing. The trick is to recycle all the bottles back from customers and hand wash them and reuse them again. The same thing Chucky Cheese does with the kids' tokens.

BABY AUK

100 WAYS TO MAKE MONEY IN PRI$ON

62. GREETING CARDS

Hand-make special cards for different occasions. Make sure they stand out and you do something to them that other card makers don't do like pop-out ones, see-through, big sizes, and etc.

63. SPECIAL SAUCES

Do you have a special ingredient that people love? Why not get paid off it? McDonald's, Checkers, pizza places, and more do it. Do the same thing in prison and watch how you blow up. Always remember it's the littlest things that count.

64. CINNAMON ROLLS

Take some bread, about 20 pieces, and break them into crumbs in a trash bag. Add about five pastry cakes. Put about 10 ounces of cinnamon into the bag or until it looks nice and brownish. Add enough water, just a little, to form it all into a big ball. Then pinch off nice pieces to form a cookie-size cinnamon roll. You can add icing or etc. to dress it up and there you have it.

65. OILS

One of my favorites. Go purchase as many oils as you can afford from canteen, then ask around or get eye drop bottles from inmates, the small ones. Next, break all the oils down into the small bottles and now you created an oil business. One big bottle of oil should make about 10 small bottles or four medium ones.

66. ASSISTANT

Okay, laugh if you want to. I'm serious. Everyone needs help to make it. Go ask around and see if someone needs a personal assistant. Let them know your skills and I can guarantee you'll take this career to the outside.

67. BATTERIES

Sell single batteries. It works and is a high demand. Open up a box and always keep them handy. Three to four stamps each. In the end you'll see what I'm talking about.

68. BUSINESS CLASSES

I'll say about 80 percent of people who come to prison don't even try to reform. They feel as though prison shut them down, but actually it hasn't. You just gotta really put in the work. If you know about real estate, stocks, buying and selling merchandise, why not charge to teach classes? It will really show how important the individual really wanna learn. Don't stress or waste your time on people who don't want to put the energy in.

69. CANDY BAGS

Get lil baggies and put different kinds of candy in it like M&Ms, Jolly Ranchers, Reese's Pieces, and etc. People love snacks, especially when you make it easy for them to purchase while they're walking the rec yard, playing cards, or watching a TV show.

70. CANDIED/CARAMEL APPLES

Apples are free. Most prisons give them away at lunch or dinnertime. So, you must ask inmates for their apples or even pay two stamps for them. You'll make it back. Collect some plastic forks and spoons because you'll break off the top and use the rest as your sticks. If you don't have little soft caramel candies to melt, use nondairy creamer and green or red Kool-Aid. Mix the three-ounce creamer and one box of Kool-Aid together in a bowl with a little water, enough to make it thick. Then you dip the apples in it. Lastly, poke the stick in the apple. Now look what you got.

71. Ice Cream

When I bought handmade ice cream in prison, I never purchased no more from canteen. It's amazing. You'll need a lot of salt, the rock salt you use for snow, and some nondairy creamer, about one bag for every 2 to 3 ice creams. Also, some milk and small baggies. Put all the creamer in a big bag, some milk, and sugar. Mix it up to your tastes and add your specialties. Then pour it into the baggies and tie them up. Sit them on ice. Please remember all the salt goes into the ice, it is what locks the ice cream up.

72. Fudge Cakes

You can do this all type of ways. There is no real way. You can take some cookies, pastry cakes, and any kind of Little Debbies. Crumble it all together in a bowl or bag. Add some water so it gets nice and doughty. Then spread it out like a big cake. Sprinkle some peanuts, Snickers, or M&Ms on top. Cut some slices and you ready to go.

73. Make Kufis

Kufis are a religious item that Muslims wear on their head who practices Islam. Some institutions sell sizes that are either too small or too big. Some only provide one or two colors. So, if you good with sewing, cutting, and etc., this is a great field to invest in.

74. Cookie Sandwiches

Easy money. Buy a pack of chocolate cookies. It should be about 18 in a pack. You mix up a nice icing with creamer, sugar, or peanut butter. You put the icing between two cookies and sprinkle some Reese's pieces, M&Ms, or candy in it and then smash the cookies together. There so, so good prices may vary around 75-cents to $1.50 each.

75. Sell Local Numbers

I know you like, how I'm gonna do that without no help? You do got help, let me show you. Put freetrial@inmatecall.com on your prison email. They will supply you with a free local number for two weeks. Then you can buy five numbers for $15. All you gotta do is keep one or two for yourself and sell the other ones for $7 to $10 each a month. All you gotta do is pay the company $15 a month.

76. Prayer Rugs

Order different prayer rugs from an Islamic bookstore. Some people have stamps but no $$ to buy them off their account. Just charge interest and help someone and you sell stamps for cash on account, plus you got extra.

77. Make Beats

Some facilities provide inmates with a music studio where they can record. So, if you're a beat maker, play piano or drums, charge for your time just like an engineer on the outside.

78. Incense

It's so many ways to make them but no matter what they all will be gone fast. Try to get some cinnamon, some straws off an extra broomstick, and cologne. Pour some cinnamon in a small bowl, add a lil, lil, lil bit of water so it's soft enough to roll up. Take lil, lil pieces and roll small three-inch sticks onto the broomstick straw. Let them dry up for about 30 minutes. Spray some oil on them and there you go.

79. Candles

Take a soda can and cut three inches off the bottom. This is where you will be pouring a lil oil in the circle piece. Then you cut a square piece out the middle of the other half. This is where you'll be entering to place your wick. Put some Vaseline in the can, enough to hold the wick which will be a mop string. The Vaseline is basically your wax. So, then you light the wick and set the first three-inch bottle piece of the can on top with a lil oil in it and watch it burn. Keep finessing it until you get real good, then you start making them to sell.

80. Outside $$ for Books

Just in case no one wants to pay your price for used books in prison, I have a service that will sell them for you and y'all split the cost. They will put the cash on your account. Write to: A Book You Want, 13 Bourne Ave., Attleboro, MA 02703.

81. Side Tutor

If you already have your high school diploma, GED, or were in college, you could be a side tutor. Find a couple students in your unit and let them know you're like a professor and can guarantee them some education benefits. Don't be afraid to charge for a skill that you worked hard to get.

82. Write A Book

Do you have a lil bit of money put up and would like to tell a sto- ry, whether it's fiction or nonfiction? Consider writing a book and re- ceive funds for the rest of your life. Yes, you gotta put in time, advertise, and etc., but it's worth it. Even self-publish. Here is a company that can help you. Write to: Cadmus Publishing, PO Box 532, Port Angeles, WA 98362, phone (651) 302-2539. Tell them you heard about them through MarMoes. They accept prison phone calls.

83. Sell Resource Lists

Always remember that you can make money off of other people. Completely legal. Write to: TCB, PO Box 1025, and order the resource prisoner list book for $17.95 plus $7 shipping/handling or if you don't have money, they will take four brand new flat books. Now here is the twist. When you get the book, write down a lot of valuable info that inmates will need to make their incarceration easier. Type you up a resource packet and sell them. Remember to always profit off anything you buy, or you will stay broke.

84. AUCTION ITEMS

I never seen this one done. Okay, it's like having a store or pawn shop but instead every week have an auction in your unit. Buy up different items through the week and let inmates make bids on the items, and the highest bidder receives the item.

85. TATTOO BOOKS

I'm not in no shape or form promoting anyone to get tattoos in prison because from my understanding you could get in trouble. But you can sell the books for artwork for those who love to draw for others. They're a hot commodity all over the system. Also, you can put some of your artwork in this book: Ink from Pen, 1440 Beaumont Ave. Suite A-2.266, Beaumont, CA 92223.

86. LOCKER BUDDIES

These are handmade cloth bags made inside your locker to hold extra stuff like hygiene, pens, glasses, and other accessories. They normally come with about 8 to 12 pockets. I'ma tell you now if you can sew then you can do this.

87. DO INMATE WILLS

No one ever plans for the future, and you can make them aware of this. If you wanna learn how to do wills while you're in prison and start to provide inmates with it for a fee, write to: E.P.S., PO Box 1717, Appleton, WI 54912-1717 and order the do-it-yourself will for $6. All you got to do is learn it and watch your investment blow up.

88. FRIEND FINDER

It's a lot of inmates who lost touch with old friends, family members, and loved ones. You can supply a service where you can find them. Have your significant other search Google or social media and locate them. You can charge three names for $10. Trust me, it works, I have done it personally myself and helped a lot of inmates. Please don't use it for criminal activity.

89. MAGAZINES

A nice lil side hustle that will create a cash flow. Just say you got an extra $75 to invest. There are magazines called Straight Stunting, Phat Puffs, Kite Magazine, Butts, and etc. of all kinds of models and gossip. Guys in prison love them. They're around $15 each and after you look at them, resell them. You can get at least double, especially when some issues are limited edition and sold out. So, just keep reinvesting and you'll never lose.

90. RECOVERY COACH

Are you a recovering addict and want to help others overcome their addiction? Write to: Parfessionals, PO Box 163, Deberry, TX 75639. You can take free courses while in prison and make a career out of it. All you have to do is invest in a lil bit of your time.

91. BUY Y.S.N. MAGAZINE

This is a new magazine called "Your Success News." It helps inmates with resources, methods, and advertising their businesses while incarcerated. It comes out bi-yearly, January and July, for $15 with shipping/handling. Every inmate should have one to keep them up to date with information that others don't expose. Send two brand new flat books of stamps or institutional check to: Ebony Akins, PO Box 70565, Toledo, OH 43607. If you're sending stamps or a letter letting them know the money is on the way or to reach out, put MarMoes as your header.

92. BOOK EDITING

Are you good with grammar and language? It's a lot of inmates who could use you to edit their fiction and nonfiction books. Come up with a price per sheet and spread the word.

93. PUBLIC SPEAKER

Not only prison but the world needs people like you. Your delivery and the way you reach the people. If you're real serious about this, try to set up a public speaking class to teach others. This is an investment in yourself for the future. You'll become so good that people will pay you for your time.

94. BITCOIN

If you haven't heard, Bitcoin is something to invest in. If you have a lil spare money and want to let your money grow while in prison and make at least 10% a year. Call (321) - 465 - 2451, ask for Chris about Buk money.

95. SHELVES/VENT COVERS

Do you know how to make shelves and vent covers? If so, why not get a lil money off of it as a side hustle? But again, please follow your prison rules and regulations.

96. PRISON-MADE NECKLACES

One thing I can tell you right now is that people are always, always looking to buy something. So, use your hands in a correct, legal way. A lot of inmates who practice religion like to get necklaces made of symbols to represent their religion, so get creative and make it happen.

97. CREATE A TEAM

This is one of the most important things to do. You can't and will not reach your full potential without building a team. See, once you get yourself together you will seek help automatically. You and your team will help each other grow. This is one of the keys to success and reaching your goals.

98. Work Bags

Who doesn't need one of these rather if you're carrying books, snacks, law work, or etc.? This is a big, big demand. So, if you know how to make work bags out of laundry bags or etc., it's a must-need.

99. Do a Booklet

Just like the booklet you're reading now that just helped you cure the disease of being broke and to change your condition, you can do the same thing. I can guarantee you that if you implement a lot of these ideas and ways, you'll be on your way to accumulating a lot of cash. Start from zero. All it takes is action and discipline. I'll even help you get started from the beginning to the end. So, take what you learned and pay it forward. Contact: MarMoes Company, PO Box 70565, Toledo, OH 43607 and tell us how this booklet has changed your condition and how we can help you.

100. God (Allah)

They say save the best for last, and I wouldn't feel right if I didn't let you know that God (Allah) is the main foundation of your life. We may not be able to control everything that happens in our life, but we can control the way we act towards it. And I can personally tell you right now that if you truly, truly get to know Him and live your life correctly, then He will send great people into your life to help you and remove those of evil.

IF YOU'RE FOCUSING ON THE LABEL, THEN PRISON WILL ALWAYS BREAK YOU.

THE END

This may be the end of this booklet but don't let it be the end of your journey. Always remember you have the power to control your destiny, so never, ever become a victim of your circumstances or situations. Just take a second right now to look around you. It's opportunities right in front of you, great people, jobs, classes, and etc. And if you still don't see it, then one thing we know for sure is you're holding one right in your hands, so please take advantage of these ideas and ways that I know 100 percent will change you financially. We are the way we think, so until you change that then your conduct will remain the same. So, I hope that "100 Ways to Make Money in Pri$on" does just that because it has done it for me and others I taught. You deserve it.

To all the people in prison who have supported me while incarcerated, thank you.

100 WAYS TO MAKE MONEY IN PRI$ON

<u>"Message Frm the Author"</u>

I grew up hustling my whole life. Back then I sold things to destroy people, but now I employ people. See the drive never stopped I just switched the product up. (All legal) You will become what you think like the most. You will become who you assocaite with the most. And once I learned how to make money become my slave I never looked back. In this book I taught you how to get the money. Be on the lookout for my new book called "Follow My Moves) then I teach you what to do with the money.

100 WAYS TO MAKE MONEY IN PRI$ON

$ "EXTRA RESOURCES" $

"UPDATED 2024"

I can honestly say that through all my years of learning about business and becoming a merchant I come to the conclusion to the conclusion that peoples biggest mistake is procrastinating. You say you want this "you say can do this and that." So what are you waitng for. Stop making excuses. Don't let being locked up in prison make you victim of your circumstances or situations. Now let me help you expand your reach from behind bars. You ready? Lets go.

<u>INMATE SERVICES</u>

These different companier will help you with internet researching, photos, and emailing.

1. 4 Ever Connected, LLC

   P.O. Box 471898

   Tulsa, OK 74147

2. A Book You Want

   P.O. Box 16141

   Rumford, RI 02916

3. A Lasting Expression

    P.O. Box 222704

    Hollywood, FL 33022

4. AB Services

    P.O. Box 1424

    Mount Vernon, IL 62864

5. Affordable Inmate Services

    P.O. Box 635145

    Nacogdoches, TX 75963

6. ATS Henderson

    544 Parkson Rd, STE F

    Hendseron, NV 89011

7. Cellmate & Convict Services

    P.O. Box 653

    Venus, TX 76048

8. eHelp4 prisoners

    539 W. Commerce St Ste. 118

    Dallas, TX 76048

9. Friends Outside

    P.O. Box 4083

    Stockton, CA 95204

10. HD Products and Services

    P.O. Box 62412

    Houston, TX 77205

11. Help From Beyond the Walls

    P.O. Box 318

    Palmyra, ME 04965

12. Help From Outside

    2620 Bellevue Way NE #200

    Bellevue, WA 98004

13. Inmate lil Helpers

    P.O. Box 4173

    Oakland, CA 91614

14. Inmates "R" US

    P.O. Box 2890

    Laurel, MO 20709 c phone #) 301-363-7555

PENPALS

It's nothing like having a great freind, or spouse by your side. You gotta just go into it with the right intensions. It's not about getting money from a pen pal or misusing them. It's about building a foundation to help each other grow mentally and spiritually.

1. Friends and Lovers Magazine

   Luigi Spatota Suite 46

   McCreary Trail Bolton, Ontario L7E 2C9 Canada

2. In Touch For Inmates

   P.O. Box 4135

   Lynchburg, VA 24502

3. Cosmic Cupid

   P.O. Box 383

   Cookeville, TN 38503

4. Conpals

   465 NE 181st Ave, 308

   Portland, OR 97230

5. Cell Pals

   P.O. Box 296

   Leonville, LA 70551

6. Christian Pen Pals

   P.O. Box 11296

   Hickory, NC 28603

7. Diversified Press

   P.O. Box 135005

   Clemont, FL 34713

8. Friends 4 Prisoners

   20770 Hwy. 28 N. STE 108-178

   San Antonio, TX 78258

9. Friends Beyond Walls Inc.

   55 Mansion St 1030

   Poughkeepsie, NY 12602

10. Human Rights Pen Pal Program

    P.O. Box 71378

    Oakland, CA 94612

11. Inmate Mingle

    P.O. Box 23207

    Columbia, SC 29224

12. Inmate Pen-pal Connection

    49 Crown St. 208

    Brooklyn, NY 11225

13. In mate House Love

    4001 Ingle wood Ave Ste 101-144

    Redondo Beach, CA 90278

14. Jail Babes

    P.O. Box 845

    Winchester, OR 97495

15. Lost Vault

    P.O. Box 242

    Mascot, TN 37808

16. Love a prisoner

    P.O. Box 192

    Deguncy, LA 70633

Inmate Websites

www.inmate.com
www.prisoninmate.com
www.prisoninmatepenpal.com
www.inmateconnection.com
www.femaleprisonpenpals.com

www.inmatemingle.com
www.loveaprisoner.com
www.convictpenpals.com
www.prisonerlife.com
www.cellpals.com

100 WAYS TO MAKE MONEY IN PRI$ON

www.convictmailbag.com

www.jewishpenpals.com

www.prisontalk.com

www.marriage88.com

www.penpalparty.com

www.hotprisonpals.com

www.askaconvict.com

www.penpalsnow.com

www. worldnation.com

www.palsforfree.com

100 Ways to
to Make Money
in Pri$on

Baby Auk

Cadmus Publishing
www.cadmuspublishing.com

Note: None of these ideas pertain to gambling, intoxication, selling/ buying illegal substances, oppressing physically or mentally to anyone. Please follow prison rules and guidelines.

Please be aware that some of these resources may have changed their address, or may not contact you A.S.A.P.

Dear Never Broke Again,

This booklet is the cure to being broke. It's a lot of people in prison who wants to see someone sink while knowing they have the power to help them. Well, guess what? Not anymore. You are now holding 100 Ways to Make Money in Prison legally all by yourself. I have personally used a lot of these ideas and actually created most of them to get me where I'm at (six figures). Yeah, you are gonna lose some friends, some even gonna laugh at you because you're not destroying yourself no more like them. I walked around prison for years following these 100 ways. Only bought what I needed, saved a lot, stayed focused, and didn't look for problems, only looked for opportunities. Your life didn't stop just because you came to prison. You just gotta stop watching TV and instead watch your account grow.

Da Prisonaire

YOU GOTTA DO WHAT'S BEST FOR YOU,
NOT THEM.

1. RENT MP3 PLAYER/MUSIC/TABLET

Just like Rent-A-center but a different kind of formula. Buy an MP3 player if you don't already have one. Purchase all the NEW music that comes out. Make sure you get gospel, R&B, rock-n-roll, and rap. You may spend about $90 - $150 for the player/tablet and buy music every two weeks after the renter pays you and brings it back. It's a lot of you right now you have music on your systems and just sit and listen to it all day and waste money on songs. Why not rent it out to someone who can't afford to purchase the whole setup?

2. ROOM SERVICE

Each dorm, unit, or housing area has at least 50 rooms/cells in it. Whether you realize it or not, we are actually living in a prison hotel. The correctional officers serve us food. If you call them, they come. Even our cells are set up like a cheap motel. But one thing they're not going to do is clean your rooms for you. So, guess what? This is where you come in. Make you a special chemical, get shampoo, a towel and wash rag. The prison already supplies you with water, a broom, and bucket. Go walk around and spread the word. Even do monthly specials where you will clean and wash a whole room four times a month. Oh yeah, and just to spice things up, spray a lil smell-good when you finish.

3. COFFEE SHOTS

It's not too many people that's incarcerated that doesn't drink coffee. A lot of guys can't even function without it or they will get a headache. I actually heard that coffee is good for the heart. We don't want to see anyone with a headache, right? So, go purchase a couple bags of coffee. I think Keefe is the most popular around $2.50 to $3.50 for a 3-ounce bag. You'll get about 40 to 50 shots using a white plastic spoon. Try not to run out because you'll never have too much. One stamp each.

4. TEXT MESSAGES

If your facility allows you to have a text messaging service, why not think like an entrepreneur and make $$ off it? I know it be a lot of inmates bothering you asking to send a text out for them. So, turn it into a business. Charge a few stamps to send a message and the reply is free. Use your customer's money to pay for your service. Make sure you let them know no illegal transactions or assaulting texts that could lead you to a disciplinary shot.

5. RAFFLE BOARD

You can become an owner in 10 minutes. No, I'm serious. Okay, listen up. Grab an all-white piece of typing paper. Draw a board of 100 squares with numbers 1 through 100. Charge $1 a square for inmates to buy, don't matter the limit of how many squares they buy. But once it's filled up, it's over with. Make sure you put their name in each square they purchase. Okay, now look. Before you start, make sure you come up with a name for your board. And at the top put "$1 wins you $60," and actually, it does because once you fill up the whole board you should have $100 in your possession. You pay the winner $60, and you keep $40. How you declare the winner is by putting all the numbers in a hat or etc. in front of everyone, and as you grab out the numbers you cross out their box on the board and the last box standing will win. You can do this two times a week.

6. SOUR TWIZZLERS

An all-time favorite. Purchase as many packs of Twizzlers you can afford. Also purchase a couple boxes of green apple Kool-Aid. It must be green apple. Now open a pack of Twizzlers. It should be around 20 in one pack. Out of one pack you should be able to cut around 65-80 pieces. Then you sprinkled one pack of Kool-Aid all over the pieces. Next you bag up about 7 to 10 pieces in each and now you're ready to distribute. Two to three stamps.

7. BANANA PUDDING

Everyone can't make banana pudding, just like everyone can't make macaroni and cheese. You got to have that special touch. But if you are that special one, then what are you waiting for? Invest in yourself. A couple small bowls, vanilla wafers, cookies, free bananas, creamer, sugar, and your secrets you'll never tell no one. Then after you're done, let it sit on ice until ready to sell. Take the $$ you make and reinvest again. Take preorders and build a damn pudding factory.

8. INSTITUTION JOB

For some reason, nobody doesn't wanna work now days. They want everything handed to them. Life doesn't work like that. Some institution jobs may pay more than others, but you gotta start at the bottom to get where you want to be. Don't focus on the pay, focus on the position you have that could possibly benefit you. For example, a kitchen job. Now you can save your food in your locker. Recreation job. Now you can work-out and learn about equipment. Yard crew. Walk around picking up trash, you also losing weight and able to advertise things you're selling. Always look for opportunities and always remember it's not always about the pay, but about the advantage your position gives you to make more money or learn from.

9. PRISON FOOT LOCKER

Just stop for a second. Look around you. I can guarantee that there's no one around you walking bare-footed. Everybody needs shoes. So, put yourself in a position to fulfill the need. Go buy up any type of shoes as long as they're not falling apart. Get different sizes, colors, work-out shoes, fancy ones, and etc. Buy low so you can make a profit. Start spreading the word that you buy used/new shoes and watch, you'll create a shoe outlet.

10. CUT HAIR

A lot of you in prison have talent but are devaluing it. If you know how to cut hair, then what are you waiting for? Let me guess. You don't have clippers. So what? Use some good razors. Guys are always looking for a trim or shape up. Start today. Let everyone know you are the new barber. It's enough room for everyone to get money, so I don't wanna hear it's already someone doing it.

11. Fix Electronics

When I first seen guys do this it blew my mind. It's like having a mechanic on the outside. If your radio, headphones, watch, or etc. is broken, take it to the guy who is good. Are you the person? Open up your shade tree cell. You'll never run out of clientele.

12. Cold Sodas

It's nothing like having a cold soda to drink, especially coming in the unit from rec or a hot sunny day or just to go with your meal. Start your business today. Get a couple cases to start off with. Make sure it's different kinds. If you don't have a bucket, special cooler, or trash bag to keep the ice in to put the sodas on, just use your sink. Most cases are around $4 to $5, so just do the math. You'll make double or more even selling at $1 to $1.50 each.

13. Nacho Dips

Game changer. Take a styrofoam tray and cut the lid off. Then you cut off the big eating part and leave only the two slots left. So, you should be left with only two sides. Put some nacho chips in both sides and some squeeze cheese on top of the chips. Quick and easy. Ready to go. Start with two cheese bottles $6 and three bags of nacho chips $6, $12 total investment.

14. Dishwasher

Laugh if you want to, but they're laughing broke. Just think about how many people eat meals a day. A lot of people are lazy or don't have time to wash their dishes. Make it your job. Break your ego.

15. Investments

Now, if you have a lil money saved on your prison account and feel the need to just sit around and do nothing, I got something for you. Wanna earn interest on it? Grab a 50-cent stamp and envelope. Write this company and say, "I want to learn more about your service." Pilgrim

Cross Group B, Port Orchard, WA 98366.

16. Stamps for Cash

You have a lot of services that are starting to let you send in brand new stamps and they will put the money on your account at their value. Here are a couple resources: 1) Great Goods, PO Box 888, Lakeworth, FL 33460; 2) P.S.E. 1077 N. Willow Ave. #107-405, Clovis, CA 93611.

17. Stocks

If you are into stocks and stopped because you're in prison or are learning about them, it's legal ways you can still buy/sell shares through mail. Here are two companies that will assist you: 1) Computer Shareholders, PO Box 505000, Louisville, KY 40233, 1-800-298-0146; 2) Bureau of the Public Debt, PO Box 7015, Parkersburg, WV 26106.

18. Sell Pen Pals

Always remember to think like an entrepreneur. I know there are a lot of great pen pals out there. People that have been in my life for years come from pen pals. Guys lose them because they try to take advantage of them or have the wrong intentions from the start. When you got a good one, hold on to him/her and help other people find one. Here is a company that sells lists of pen pals. You can order the lists and sell them individually and become known as the matchmaker. Their address is: PO Box 2515, Nyssa, OR 97913. Send $6 or one book of stamps.

19. Workout Memberships

If you have experience and methods on how to help people lose weight, all you have to do is start your own workout class. Charge each inmate by the month around $15 to $20. You must supply healthy snacks, drinks, and prison equipment like weight bags and etc., and before you know it, you'll have a waiting list!

20. IRON CLOTHES

Prison Fly is what they call someone who is always creased up 24/7 for pics, visits, or daily. You can become the cleaners. Make a special spray for starch and schedule dates inmates have occasions. They may look good wearing it, but you is the man who made it happen.

21. PHONE MESSAGES

Do you not realize that you only get between 10 to 15 minutes on the phone? So, in order to deliver a message for someone is taking your time. So, charge them an item or couple of stamps. It's like shipping and handling. You're shipping your time and handling their business.

22. COMEDIAN

No, I am actually serious. Are you a natural-born funny person or have funny prison stories? Well, you can make $$ off it. Write to: Mr. Story, PO Box 60903, Philadelphia, PA 19133, and if he uses or likes your funny stories, they will pay you for it.

23. ENTERTAINER

If you're a movie writer or want to get your voice heard and have no $$ to start with, don't worry. Contact UBF Scholarship Foundation, PO Box 862, Bristow, OK 74010-1010. They're a nonprofit looking to put the funds up for inmates. The founder is a prisoner himself.

24. SELLING/LICENSING IDEAS

Do you have an idea or product you want to sell or license, but because you're in prison you can't effectively market it? Write to: American Intellectual Property Law Association, 2001 Jefferson Davis Highway Suite 203, Arlington, VA 22202.

25. BUILDING GROWTH

I love this service. They help you with inmate banking, building credit, cash app, and re-entry. So, if you're on your way home soon and need resources, this is who you need to contact. And yes, they do all this and more while you're incarcerated. Write to: J.K.C. 1140 Cornell Street, Scranton, PA 18504.

26. LAW WORK

You know it's more than 2.3 million people locked up in the U.S., more than any other country. Also, more than half the cases have errors in them, and 15 percent have been getting out wrongly convicted after doing 15 or more years. If you have experience with codes and rights, what are you waiting for? People need your help and are wiling to pay for their freedom and justice. Become the prison lawyer and before you know it, you'll have a law firm inside the walls.

BAD COMPANY WILL CORRUPT GOOD CHARACTER.

27. TAFFY CANDY

The hottest commodity in prison. A quick rundown—one bag of nondairy creamer and around 8 to 10 packs of Kool-Aid. Poor the three-ounce creamer into a bag with the Kool-Aid and mix it around. Keep adding half a teaspoon of water into the mix until it's a nice kinda hard texture. Spread it out flat and cut around 100 pieces. One stamp apiece gets you about $30 off a $5 investment.

28. SUCKERS (BLOW POPS)

A great demand. You gonna need about 10 empty pill bottles, a bag of Jolly Ranchers or hard fruit candies, and some Q-Tips. Put three pieces of candy in each pill bottle, then you put the bottles in the microwave with the lids off, five at a time. Keep stopping the timer and look every 10 seconds until the candy melts. Next, take them out and stick the Q-Tips in while it's soft, then hold the sticks until the candy hardens. Lastly, pop the sucker out. $1 to $2 each.

29. THE BREAKDOWN (CHIPS)

I actually believe I was the first inmate to actually breakdown chips. Some people can't afford to buy a whole bag, so I made it to where they could be satisfied also. Just get different kinds and put a handful in little sandwich baggies. You should get about 6 to 8 small baggies out a big bag. At 2-3 stamps each you'll become big. Trust me.

30. RESELL BOOKS

Why would you buy information and then give it away? No, you sell the information as well once you get everything out of it you wanted. People misuse books all the time, so let them do it with their time, not yours. If you keep buying them and then give them away, you just became a dependent.

31. SELL COLD MILKS

Milks are free, issued out every morning at breakfast, so get up early and collect them. Bring them back to the unit and put on ice. A lot of guys don't get up so early, so make sure you have the milk for their cereal when they get up or for the ones who don't like to walk up to the hall.

32. BREAKFAST (IHOP)

The early bird gets the worm. Set it up so you can have eggs, bacon, grits, bread, and etc. Make breakfast sandwiches and give your customers an orange Hi-C drink on the side.

33. FRIED WRAPS

Quick and easy to serve. Rice, meat, cheese, vegetables, sauces, and etc. Always keep them hot and tasty. A $15 investment makes you $45. Twenty tortillas. You must stay consistent.

34. PRISON CHEF

You could either cook food and sell it or cook for other people and charge them, but they must bring all the items to make it. Start you a restaurant and take orders three times a week. Hire you some help and get to work. Why waste your talent when you can get paid off something you love to do anyways?

35. PRISON HUT (PIZZA)

It is nothing like a loaded pizza with all type of toppings. I have literally tasted a pizza that would put Papa John's out of business. See, you have individuals that only know how to make certain food. Make you a dough, some use bread, crackers, or etc. Get seasonings, sauce, cheeses, meats, vegetables, and a formula you keep a secret. Take orders and also do free delivery.

36. HAND CRAFT

If you make picture frames, cars, boats, animals, or etc. I have the right service for you. They will purchase your items and put the funds on your account. A contract also has to be signed. Write to: Sticks From the Yard, 2283 Sunset Drive, Wickliffe, OH 44092.

37. SEW CLOTHES

Do you know how to sew? If so, go buy a needle and thread from commissary. It should run you no more than $5. Make you a little written flyer and let people know your prices and etc. The inmates need you. Quit thinking you don't have a way to benefit yourself and others.

38. LAUNDROMAT

I know every facility will wash your laundry for free, but just look how they come back. Wrinkled, shrunken, and no smell good. It's nothing wrong with washing clothes. A lil secret—the washing machine is actually washing it, all you're doing is watching it, making sure it gets dried and folded. Use some good washing powder and charge by the week. (WOW)

39. WASH SHOES

Good soap, shampoo, new toothbrush to scrub, and towel. Buy some shoe polish just in case they need it. Turn bad into good and you're in business.

40. PAWN SHOP

The biggest business I ever started in prison. You want to buy low items so you can also sell cheap items. Anything that I saw with value I purchased or made value out of it. If customers pawned something and didn't pay the low interest in one week, you keep it. Remember to be fair and just.

41. TYPE CONTRACTS

Dealing with a lot of businesses and agreements rather for court or power of attorneys, you'll need some kind of contracts. So, if you know how to type let your fingers make you money.

42. BRAID HAIR

Whoever said this is a female job is a lie. This is a great, great hustle and a must-need in prison. If you know how to braid or do dreads, don't hide it. Let it be known and stack your commissary and account up. Even give monthly specials.

43. BODEGA

How can we survive without a small store around? Become an owner today. Just start small and you will grow huge. A lot of people fail at it because they don't understand supply, demand, bookkeeping, pay yourself, saving, and being a people's person all played a part of their downfall. Don't let that be you. I went from $50 to starting outside businesses off a prison bodega and so can you.

44. SELL PICTURES

Who doesn't like exclusive pics of Instagram models or etc.? Here are two services that sell cheap pics in bulk and you can resell them to fit someone's desire. Write to: 1) Kill Shot King, PO Box 81074, Corpus Christi, Tx 78468; 2) Free Prints App - Get the most popular Instagram Pics and have loved ones send them to you. They sell like hotcakes.

45. LIL JUICYS

Make you a big pitcher of Kool-Aid, about 10 ounces or more. Make sure it's nice and tasty. Get you some small baggies and pour the Kool-Aid in each one. Make sure you can tie them up okay so when it's done sit them on ice and in 20 minutes you got lil juicys.

46. ALL HYGIENE

Just like a bodega, but instead just stick to all cosmetics. Less complicated and people know where to buy only hygiene.

47. THE COPIER

Just wait until they see this idea. Go buy a couple copy cards around $6 to $7 each. You get 50 copies on each card. Spread the word you charge two stamps a copy, includes shipping/handling. Even give specials when you copy five or more pages. You'll triple your money and become the copy man/woman.

48. SINGLE COOKIES

It's just something about breaking things down. You'll see. Go buy some packs or bag of cookies. It has to be at least 18 or more single cookies in the bag in order to break down. Put 3 or 4 in little baggies and distribute them nonstop. Two to three stamps each.

49. POPCORN

Either buy cheddar popcorn or the microwave kind. It will be great if you had both. Get lil baggies and put both kinds together in the lil baggie and get ready to advertise your butter and cheddar enterprise. At 3 stamps each you'll kill 'em.

50. BROWNIES

I promise you it's so, so simple. Find some hot cocoa mix off commissary. A box is around $2. Put about four packs in a big bowl. Add some milk, just enough to make it thick, but still soft. Put the bowl into the microwave and watch it rise up like a cake. Keep your eye on it. Take it out, put peanuts or etc. on it. Cut into slices and your new business just started.

WE ALL CAN HAVE THE SAME
GOAL, BUT IT'S OUR MISSION THAT
SEPARATES US.

51. WRITE POEMS

Are you a great poem writer? If so, get paid and published in articles. Here are two resources to enter into contests and more: 1) Poete Maudit, PO Box 216, Farmersville, CA 93223; 2) Pen America Writing Program, 588 Broadway Suite 303, New York, NY 10012.

52. SELL ARTWORK

Sometimes inmates in prison don't want to pay your prices. Don't devalue yourself. Deal with services on the outside who will purchase your work from prison. Write to: Creative Freedom, PO Box 119, Williamson, WV 25661.

53. GHOST WRITER

Just like the music industry but instead do it for prisoners. People need poems, letters, grievances, and more written up. So, if you're good with your words and speech, we need you. Start letting it be known ASAP.

54. CROCHET

If you don't already know how to do it, you might as well learn. Invest $7 to buy a 35-page booklet for beginners at: E.P.S., PO Box 1717, Appleton, WI 54912, and start making money.

55. DRAW PORTRAITS

It takes time but as an artist your time is valuable. Inmates love to get portraits of loved ones, kids, and etc., and if you don't know how you can always purchase books to teach you.

56. FANCY ENVELOPES

Simple hustle. Buy a box of all-white envelopes (50-count) around $2. Trace or draw some nice designs and characters on al of them. Put one stamp on them and sell the envelopes around 4 to 5 stamps pre-stamped and fancy.

57. EYE COVERS

Guess what? You can make money off people's sleep. Just start making eye covers. For some reason, just covering your eyes really relaxes you. I use mine every night.

58. SHARK TANK

Yes, you have a lot of entrepreneurs all around you. Some are even willing to invest in some of these ideas if you show them you're serious and have a nice plan to pay them back. And vice-versa with the sharks who are looking to invest in a prisoner. Don't take advantage of them, that's a sign of weakness. If you do it correctly, you'll both benefit.

59. PILLOWS

Only if your unit or etc. allows you to have one, you could be the one to provide a cotton pillow for inmates. Some COs take them, some don't, so if you're the pillow man/woman, I guess it's more money for you.

60. TOOTSIE ROLLS

Game changer. Let me show you. Buy some hot cocoa mix and one bag of nondairy creamer. Pour about four packs of cocoa mix and the bag of creamer all in one trash bag (a small bag). Mix it all up then put lil by lil teaspoons of water in it until it gets hard. Keep pressing the bag and spreading it until it's smooth. Then cut up nice pieces like Tootsie Rolls (60 to 80 pieces). One stamp each.

61. BOTTLES OF KOOL-AID

Go buy a case of water. Empty all the water into one big container. Put about one box of Kool-Aid into the container also. Basically, make you some good, sweet Kool-Aid. Now all the empty water bottles you have, fill up the bottles. Put the bottles on ice and do your thing. The trick is to recycle all the bottles back from customers and hand wash them and reuse them again. The same thing Chucky Cheese does with the kids' tokens.

BABY AUK

100 WAYS TO MAKE MONEY IN PRI$ON

62. GREETING CARDS

Hand-make special cards for different occasions. Make sure they stand out and you do something to them that other card makers don't do like pop-out ones, see-through, big sizes, and etc.

63. SPECIAL SAUCES

Do you have a special ingredient that people love? Why not get paid off it? McDonald's, Checkers, pizza places, and more do it. Do the same thing in prison and watch how you blow up. Always remember it's the littlest things that count.

64. CINNAMON ROLLS

Take some bread, about 20 pieces, and break them into crumbs in a trash bag. Add about five pastry cakes. Put about 10 ounces of cinnamon into the bag or until it looks nice and brownish. Add enough water, just a little, to form it all into a big ball. Then pinch off nice pieces to form a cookie-size cinnamon roll. You can add icing or etc. to dress it up and there you have it.

65. OILS

One of my favorites. Go purchase as many oils as you can afford from canteen, then ask around or get eye drop bottles from inmates, the small ones. Next, break all the oils down into the small bottles and now you created an oil business. One big bottle of oil should make about 10 small bottles or four medium ones.

66. ASSISTANT

Okay, laugh if you want to. I'm serious. Everyone needs help to make it. Go ask around and see if someone needs a personal assistant. Let them know your skills and I can guarantee you'll take this career to the outside.

67. BATTERIES

Sell single batteries. It works and is a high demand. Open up a box and always keep them handy. Three to four stamps each. In the end you'll see what I'm talking about.

68. BUSINESS CLASSES

I'll say about 80 percent of people who come to prison don't even try to reform. They feel as though prison shut them down, but actually it hasn't. You just gotta really put in the work. If you know about real estate, stocks, buying and selling merchandise, why not charge to teach classes? It will really show how important the individual really wanna learn. Don't stress or waste your time on people who don't want to put the energy in.

69. CANDY BAGS

Get lil baggies and put different kinds of candy in it like M&Ms, Jolly Ranchers, Reese's Pieces, and etc. People love snacks, especially when you make it easy for them to purchase while they're walking the rec yard, playing cards, or watching a TV show.

70. CANDIED/CARAMEL APPLES

Apples are free. Most prisons give them away at lunch or dinnertime. So, you must ask inmates for their apples or even pay two stamps for them. You'll make it back. Collect some plastic forks and spoons because you'll break off the top and use the rest as your sticks. If you don't have little soft caramel candies to melt, use nondairy creamer and green or red Kool-Aid. Mix the three-ounce creamer and one box of Kool-Aid together in a bowl with a little water, enough to make it thick. Then you dip the apples in it. Lastly, poke the stick in the apple. Now look what you got.

71. ICE CREAM

When I bought handmade ice cream in prison, I never purchased no more from canteen. It's amazing. You'll need a lot of salt, the rock salt you use for snow, and some nondairy creamer, about one bag for every 2 to 3 ice creams. Also, some milk and small baggies. Put all the creamer in a big bag, some milk, and sugar. Mix it up to your tastes and add your specialties. Then pour it into the baggies and tie them up. Sit them on ice. Please remember all the salt goes into the ice, it is what locks the ice cream up.

72. FUDGE CAKES

You can do this all type of ways. There is no real way. You can take some cookies, pastry cakes, and any kind of Little Debbies. Crumble it all together in a bowl or bag. Add some water so it gets nice and doughty. Then spread it out like a big cake. Sprinkle some peanuts, Snickers, or M&Ms on top. Cut some slices and you ready to go.

73. MAKE KUFIS

Kufis are a religious item that Muslims wear on their head who practices Islam. Some institutions sell sizes that are either too small or too big. Some only provide one or two colors. So, if you good with sewing, cutting, and etc., this is a great field to invest in.

74. COOKIE SANDWICHES

Easy money. Buy a pack of chocolate cookies. It should be about 18 in a pack. You mix up a nice icing with creamer, sugar, or peanut butter. You put the icing between two cookies and sprinkle some Reese's pieces, M&Ms, or candy in it and then smash the cookies together. There so, so good prices may vary around 75-cents to $1.50 each.

75. SELL LOCAL NUMBERS

I know you like, how I'm gonna do that without no help? You do got help, let me show you. Put freetrial@inmatecall.com on your prison email. They will supply you with a free local number for two weeks. Then you can buy five numbers for $15. All you gotta do is keep one or two for yourself and sell the other ones for $7 to $10 each a month. All you gotta do is pay the company $15 a month.

76. PRAYER RUGS

Order different prayer rugs from an Islamic bookstore. Some people have stamps but no $$ to buy them off their account. Just charge interest and help someone and you sell stamps for cash on account, plus you got extra.

77. MAKE BEATS

Some facilities provide inmates with a music studio where they can record. So, if you're a beat maker, play piano or drums, charge for your time just like an engineer on the outside.

78. INCENSE

It's so many ways to make them but no matter what they all will be gone fast. Try to get some cinnamon, some straws off an extra broomstick, and cologne. Pour some cinnamon in a small bowl, add a lil, lil, lil bit of water so it's soft enough to roll up. Take lil, lil pieces and roll small three-inch sticks onto the broomstick straw. Let them dry up for about 30 minutes. Spray some oil on them and there you go.

79. CANDLES

Take a soda can and cut three inches off the bottom. This is where you will be pouring a lil oil in the circle piece. Then you cut a square piece out the middle of the other half. This is where you'll be entering to place your wick. Put some Vaseline in the can, enough to hold the wick which will be a mop string. The Vaseline is basically your wax. So, then you light the wick and set the first three-inch bottle piece of the can on top with a lil oil in it and watch it burn. Keep finessing it until you get real good, then you start making them to sell.

80. Outside $$ for Books

Just in case no one wants to pay your price for used books in prison, I have a service that will sell them for you and y'all split the cost. They will put the cash on your account. Write to: A Book You Want, 13 Bourne Ave., Attleboro, MA 02703.

81. Side Tutor

If you already have your high school diploma, GED, or were in college, you could be a side tutor. Find a couple students in your unit and let them know you're like a professor and can guarantee them some education benefits. Don't be afraid to charge for a skill that you worked hard to get.

82. Write a Book

Do you have a lil bit of money put up and would like to tell a sto- ry, whether it's fiction or nonfiction? Consider writing a book and re- ceive funds for the rest of your life. Yes, you gotta put in time, advertise, and etc., but it's worth it. Even self-publish. Here is a company that can help you. Write to: Cadmus Publishing, PO Box 532, Port Angeles, WA 98362, phone (651) 302-2539. Tell them you heard about them through MarMoes. They accept prison phone calls.

83. Sell Resource Lists

Always remember that you can make money off of other people. Completely legal. Write to: TCB, PO Box 1025, and order the resource prisoner list book for $17.95 plus $7 shipping/handling or if you don't have money, they will take four brand new flat books. Now here is the twist. When you get the book, write down a lot of valuable info that inmates will need to make their incarceration easier. Type you up a resource packet and sell them. Remember to always profit off anything you buy, or you will stay broke.

84. AUCTION ITEMS

I never seen this one done. Okay, it's like having a store or pawn shop but instead every week have an auction in your unit. Buy up different items through the week and let inmates make bids on the items, and the highest bidder receives the item.

85. TATTOO BOOKS

I'm not in no shape or form promoting anyone to get tattoos in prison because from my understanding you could get in trouble. But you can sell the books for artwork for those who love to draw for others. They're a hot commodity all over the system. Also, you can put some of your artwork in this book: Ink from Pen, 1440 Beaumont Ave. Suite A-2.266, Beaumont, CA 92223.

86. LOCKER BUDDIES

These are handmade cloth bags made inside your locker to hold extra stuff like hygiene, pens, glasses, and other accessories. They normally come with about 8 to 12 pockets. I'ma tell you now if you can sew then you can do this.

87. DO INMATE WILLS

No one ever plans for the future, and you can make them aware of this. If you wanna learn how to do wills while you're in prison and start to provide inmates with it for a fee, write to: E.P.S., PO Box 1717, Appleton, WI 54912-1717 and order the do-it-yourself will for $6. All you got to do is learn it and watch your investment blow up.

88. Friend Finder

It's a lot of inmates who lost touch with old friends, family members, and loved ones. You can supply a service where you can find them. Have your significant other search Google or social media and locate them. You can charge three names for $10. Trust me, it works, I have done it personally myself and helped a lot of inmates. Please don't use it for criminal activity.

89. Magazines

A nice lil side hustle that will create a cash flow. Just say you got an extra $75 to invest. There are magazines called Straight Stunting, Phat Puffs, Kite Magazine, Butts, and etc. of all kinds of models and gossip. Guys in prison love them. They're around $15 each and after you look at them, resell them. You can get at least double, especially when some issues are limited edition and sold out. So, just keep reinvesting and you'll never lose.

90. Recovery Coach

Are you a recovering addict and want to help others overcome their addiction? Write to: Parfessionals, PO Box 163, Deberry, TX 75639. You can take free courses while in prison and make a career out of it. All you have to do is invest in a lil bit of your time.

91. Buy Y.S.N. Magazine

This is a new magazine called "Your Success News." It helps inmates with resources, methods, and advertising their businesses while incarcerated. It comes out bi-yearly, January and July, for $15 with shipping/handling. Every inmate should have one to keep them up to date with information that others don't expose. Send two brand new flat books of stamps or institutional check to: Ebony Akins, PO Box 70565, Toledo, OH 43607. If you're sending stamps or a letter letting them know the money is on the way or to reach out, put MarMoes as your header.

92. BOOK EDITING

Are you good with grammar and language? It's a lot of inmates who could use you to edit their fiction and nonfiction books. Come up with a price per sheet and spread the word.

93. PUBLIC SPEAKER

Not only prison but the world needs people like you. Your delivery and the way you reach the people. If you're real serious about this, try to set up a public speaking class to teach others. This is an investment in yourself for the future. You'll become so good that people will pay you for your time.

94. BITCOIN

If you haven't heard, Bitcoin is something to invest in. If you have a lil spare money and want to let your money grow while in prison and make at least 10% a year. Call (321) - 465 - 2451, ask for Chris about Buk money.

95. SHELVES/VENT COVERS

Do you know how to make shelves and vent covers? If so, why not get a lil money off of it as a side hustle? But again, please follow your prison rules and regulations.

96. PRISON-MADE NECKLACES

One thing I can tell you right now is that people are always, always looking to buy something. So, use your hands in a correct, legal way. A lot of inmates who practice religion like to get necklaces made of symbols to represent their religion, so get creative and make it happen.

97. CREATE A TEAM

This is one of the most important things to do. You can't and will not reach your full potential without building a team. See, once you get yourself together you will seek help automatically. You and your team will help each other grow. This is one of the keys to success and reaching your goals.

98. WORK BAGS

Who doesn't need one of these rather if you're carrying books, snacks, law work, or etc.? This is a big, big demand. So, if you know how to make work bags out of laundry bags or etc., it's a must-need.

99. DO A BOOKLET

Just like the booklet you're reading now that just helped you cure the disease of being broke and to change your condition, you can do the same thing. I can guarantee you that if you implement a lot of these ideas and ways, you'll be on your way to accumulating a lot of cash. Start from zero. All it takes is action and discipline. I'll even help you get started from the beginning to the end. So, take what you learned and pay it forward. Contact: MarMoes Company, PO Box 70565, Toledo, OH 43607 and tell us how this booklet has changed your condition and how we can help you.

100. GOD (ALLAH)

They say save the best for last, and I wouldn't feel right if I didn't let you know that God (Allah) is the main foundation of your life. We may not be able to control everything that happens in our life, but we can control the way we act towards it. And I can personally tell you right now that if you truly, truly get to know Him and live your life correctly, then He will send great people into your life to help you and remove those of evil.

IF YOU'RE FOCUSING ON THE LABEL,
THEN PRISON WILL ALWAYS BREAK
YOU.

The End

This may be the end of this booklet but don't let it be the end of your journey. Always remember you have the power to control your destiny, so never, ever become a victim of your circumstances or situations. Just take a second right now to look around you. It's opportunities right in front of you, great people, jobs, classes, and etc. And if you still don't see it, then one thing we know for sure is you're holding one right in your hands, so please take advantage of these ideas and ways that I know 100 percent will change you financially. We are the way we think, so until you change that then your conduct will remain the same. So, I hope that "100 Ways to Make Money in Pri$on" does just that because it has done it for me and others I taught. You deserve it.

To all the people in prison who have supported me while incarcerated, thank you.

"Message Frm the Author"

I grew up hustling my whole life. Back then I sold things to destroy people, but now I employ people. See the drive never stopped I just switched the product up. (All legal) You will become what you think like the most. You will become who you assocaite with the most. And once I learned how to make money become my slave I never looked back. In this book I taught you how to get the money. Be on the lookout for my new book called "Follow My Moves) then I teach you what to do with the money.

$ "EXTRA RESOURCES" $

"UPDATED 2024"

I can honestly say that through all my years of learning about business and becoming a merchant I come to the conclusion to the conclusion that peoples biggest mistake is procrastinating. You say you want this "you say can do this and that." So what are you waitng for. Stop making excuses. Don't let being locked up in prison make you victim of your circumstances or situations. Now let me help you expand your reach from behind bars. You ready? Lets go.

INMATE SERVICES

These different companier will help you with internet researching, photos, and emailing.

1. 4 Ever Connected, LLC

   P.O. Box 471898

   Tulsa, OK 74147

2. A Book You Want

   P.O. Box 16141

   Rumford, RI 02916

3. A Lasting Expression

   P.O. Box 222704

   Hollywood, FL 33022

4. AB Services

   P.O. Box 1424

   Mount Vernon, IL 62864

5. Affordable Inmate Services

   P.O. Box 635145

   Nacogdoches, TX 75963

6. ATS Henderson

   544 Parkson Rd, STE F

   Hendseron, NV 89011

7. Cellmate & Convict Services

   P.O. Box 653

   Venus, TX 76048

8. eHelp4 prisoners

   539 W. Commerce St Ste. 118

   Dallas, TX 76048

9. Friends Outside

    P.O. Box 4083

    Stockton, CA 95204

10. HD Products and Services

    P.O. Box 62412

    Houston, TX 77205

11. Help From Beyond the Walls

    P.O. Box 318

    Palmyra, ME 04965

12. Help From Outside

    2620 Bellevue Way NE #200

    Bellevue, WA 98004

13. Inmate lil Helpers

    P.O. Box 4173

    Oakland, CA 91614

14. Inmates "R" US

    P.O. Box 2890

    Laurel, MO 20709 c phone #) 301-363-7555

PENPALS

It's nothing like having a great freind, or spouse by your side. You gotta just go into it with the right intensions. It's not about getting money from a pen pal or misusing them. It's about building a foundation to help each other grow mentally and spiritually.

1. Friends and Lovers Magazine

   Luigi Spatota Suite 46

   McCreary Trail Bolton, Ontario L7E 2C9 Canada

2. In Touch For Inmates

   P.O. Box 4135

   Lynchburg, VA 24502

3. Cosmic Cupid

   P.O. Box 383

   Cookeville, TN 38503

4. Conpals

   465 NE 181st Ave, 308

   Portland, OR 97230

5. Cell Pals

   P.O. Box 296

   Leonville, LA 70551

6. Christian Pen Pals

    P.O. Box 11296

    Hickory, NC 28603

7. Diversified Press

    P.O. Box 135005

    Clemont, FL 34713

8. Friends 4 Prisoners

    20770 Hwy. 28 N. STE 108-178

    San Antonio, TX 78258

9. Friends Beyond Walls Inc.

    55 Mansion St 1030

    Poughkeepsie, NY 12602

10. Human Rights Pen Pal Program

    P.O. Box 71378

    Oakland, CA 94612

11. Inmate Mingle

    P.O. Box 23207

    Columbia, SC 29224

12. Inmate Pen-pal Connection

    49 Crown St. 208

    Brooklyn, NY 11225

13. In mate House Love

    4001 Ingle wood Ave Ste 101-144

    Redondo Beach, CA 90278

14. Jail Babes

    P.O. Box 845

    Winchester, OR 97495

15. Lost Vault

    P.O. Box 242

    Mascot, TN 37808

16. Love a prisoner

    P.O. Box 192

    Deguncy, LA 70633

Inmate Websites

www.inmate.com
www.prisoninmate.com
www.prisoninmatepenpal.com
www.inmateconnection.com
www.femaleprisonpenpals.com

www.inmatemingle.com
www.loveaprisoner.com
www.convictpenpals.com
www.prisonerlife.com
www.cellpals.com

100 WAYS TO MAKE MONEY IN PRI$ON

www.convictmailbag.com

www.jewishpenpals.com

www.prisontalk.com

www.marriage88.com

www.penpalparty.com

www.hotprisonpals.com

www.askaconvict.com

www.penpalsnow.com

www. worldnation.com

www.palsforfree.com

BABY AUK

Made in the USA
Monee, IL
27 September 2024

66780971R00059